TOP THAT! * ACTIVITY * FUN * LEARNING

Junior
How to Draw
Baby Animals

Published by Top That! Publishing plc
Tide Mill Way, Woodbridge, Suffolk, IP12 1AP, UK
www.topthatpublishing.com
Copyright © 2013 Top That! Publishing plc
All rights reserved.
0 2 4 6 8 9 7 5 3 1
Printed and bound in China

Introduction

Have you always wanted to draw kittens, puppies, lambs and other baby animals, but were put off because they looked too difficult? Have no fear! This book shows you a fun and easy way to draw all kinds of baby animals.

Just follow the tips and step-by-step instructions, and you'll soon learn a set of basic drawing techniques that you can then apply to any subject.

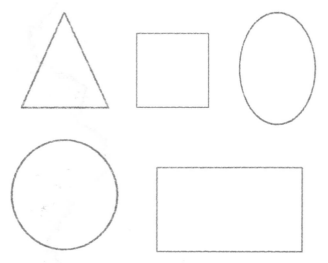

Basic Shapes

When you want to draw an object, a good way to start is to look at the object carefully and to break it down in your mind into a series of simple shapes—triangles, squares, rectangles, circles and ovals.

Top Tip!

To draw good, clear lines, you need to keep your pencils nice and sharp with a pencil sharpener.

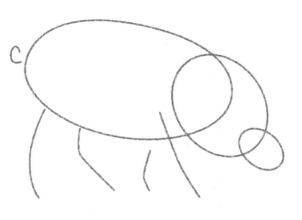

Animals tend to break down mostly into ovals and circles, with additional curved lines for arms, legs and tails (as shown above).

Notice which shapes are bigger or smaller than others, and where they join together. Look carefully at their angles and proportions. Spend time just looking before you pick up your pencil!

Tools of the Trade

You will need a pencil, an eraser, a pencil sharpener, a ruler, a fine black marker pen and fiber-tip pens or pencils for coloring in your drawings.

2

Four Simple Steps

You can apply the "basic shapes" technique to drawing any subject, including baby animals. You can use it for simple front-on and side-on views, as well as for more complicated angled views. All it takes is four simple steps...

Top Tip!

Sketch your pencil guidelines lightly, otherwise, when you come to erase them, you will see traces of them on the finished drawing.

Step 1. First, break the animal down into its basic shapes.

Step 2. Next, sketch a simple outline using the shapes as guidelines.

Step 3. Build up the detail, go over your sketch in pen and erase the guidelines.

Step 4. Finally add color to bring your picture to life!

Drawing Faces Front-on

If you are drawing an animal's face front-on, both halves need to look the same. The best way to achieve this is to lightly sketch a cross on the face as a guide. Position the eyes on the horizontal line of the cross. The vertical line is called the "line of symmetry," and the features should be exactly the same on both sides of this line.

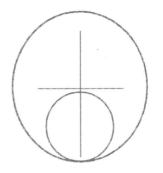

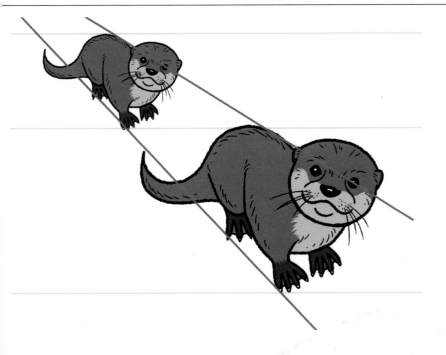

Perspective

Many of the drawings in this book show baby animals seen from an angle. When you look at a drawing, it should be obvious where the artist was in relation to what was being drawn. This is known as "perspective."

The basic rule of perspective is that things in the distance appear smaller than those closer to the viewer.

Kittens

To start with, try drawing these playful kittens in four different poses!

Top Tip!
Think carefully about where to sketch the cross on your animal's face. The position will change if the animal is looking up or down, or its face is tilted.

Side-on View

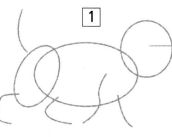

Step 1. Sketch a circle for the head. Add a horizontal line as a guide for the position of the eyes. Next, sketch two ovals for the body. Add lines for the legs and tail, copying the angles shown here.

Step 2. Draw the kitten's outline around your guidelines. Then add the ears, eye, nose and mouth.

Step 3. Add a few dots for whiskers and curved lines for toes. Then go over your pencil outline in black pen. Erase the pencil guidelines.

Step 4. Finally have fun coloring in your kitty!

Front-on View

Step 1. Sketch a circle for the head. Add a cross as a position guide for the eyes and nose (draw it slightly slanting, as the head is tilted). Then sketch three ovals for the body and feet, and lines for the legs and tail.

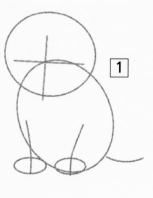

Step 2. Draw the kitten's outline around your guidelines, adding the ears and two back feet. Then sketch the face. Notice that the eyes are halfway down the face.

Step 4. Color in your stripy orange kitten, leaving white highlights in the eyes.

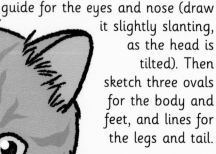

Step 3. Add detail to the feet and face—in this drawing, the cat's pupils are crescent-shaped. Then go over your outline in black pen, using short strokes to suggest fur. Erase the pencil guidelines.

Playing

Step 1. First sketch a circle for the head. Add a slanting cross as a position guide for the eyes and nose. Then overlap an oval for the body. Add lines for the legs and tail, copying the angles shown here.

Step 2. Draw the kitten's outline. Keep the head quite flat across the top, and notice that because the kitten is looking down, its mouth breaks out of the circle.

Step 3. Add detail to the face and feet, and then, in black pen, go around the outline making short strokes to suggest fur. Erase the pencil guidelines.

Step 4. Color in your playful little kitten.

Sleeping

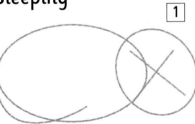

Step 1. Lightly sketch an oval and cross for the head, as shown. Overlap another oval for the body and add a line for the tail.

Step 2. Draw the kitten's outline around your guidelines. Start with the tail and back, then do the ears and face—use the cross as a position guide for the eyes and nose. Finally, draw the legs and feet.

Step 3. Build up the detail by shaping the eyes and adding whiskers, toes and foot pads. Use short strokes around the ears and body to suggest fur. Then go over your outline in black pen. Finally, erase the pencil guidelines.

Step 4. Color in your sleepy kitten and give it wavy markings.

5

Puppies

These gorgeous puppies are not only cute, but fun to draw!

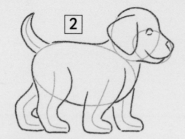

Step 1. Sketch two overlapping ovals for the head, and a guideline for the eyes. Next, sketch an oval for the body and lines for the legs and tail.

Step 2. Draw your puppy's outline around the guidelines and sketch in the face.

Step 3. Build up the detail, adding an eyebrow, dots for whiskers, and toes. Use short strokes to suggest fur. Then go over your outline in black pen. Finally, erase any pencil guidelines.

Fact File

For the first few weeks, puppies spend most of their time sleeping and drinking milk. At two to five weeks, they begin to walk.

Labrador Side-on

Step 4. Complete your puppy by coloring it in with pens or pencils.

Labrador Front-on

Step 1. First, create your guidelines by following the example shown here. Start with the head, then draw the body and legs.

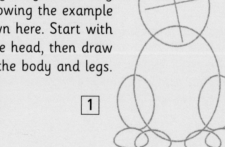

Step 4. Finally, add color to your puppy. Don't forget to highlight the eyes and nose with white circles.

Step 2. Next, sketch the outline and face. Draw the head slightly tilted, and give your puppy large eyes.

Step 3. Add toes, eyebrows, nostrils and dots for whiskers. Use short strokes on the chest and legs to suggest fur. Then go over your pencil lines in black pen and erase the guidelines.

Basset Hound

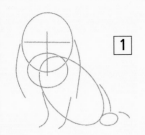

Step 1. Create your guidelines by following the example above.

Step 2. Draw the puppy's outline around your guidelines.

Step 3. Add details, such as eyebrows and fur, using short strokes. Go over your outline in black pen and erase the pencil guidelines.

Step 4. Color in your droopy-eared puppy!

Pug

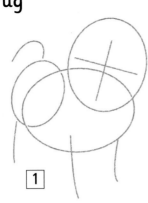

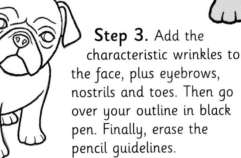

Step 1. Start by sketching an oval for the head, with a guideline cross for the eyes and nose. Next, draw two overlapping ovals for the body. Add lines for the legs and tail.

Step 2. Starting with the head, go around your guidelines drawing the pug's outline shape. Then sketch in the face using the cross as a guide.

Step 3. Add the characteristic wrinkles to the face, plus eyebrows, nostrils and toes. Then go over your outline in black pen. Finally, erase the pencil guidelines.

Step 4. Bring your bold little puppy to life by coloring him in!

Yorkshire Terrier

Step 1. For this puppy, start by sketching two ovals for the head, one for the body, and lines for the legs.

Step 2. Draw the puppy's outline around your guidelines, and sketch in the main facial features.

Step 3. Add eyebrows, toes and lots of short strokes to suggest fur. On the face, draw the fur lines radiating out from the nose. Go over your outline in black pen, and then erase the pencil guidelines.

Step 4. Color in your perky puppy in various shades of brown.

Foal

Try your hand at these gentle foals.

Angled View

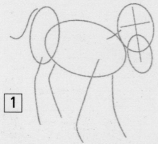

Step 1. Start by sketching two overlapping ovals for the head and two for the body. Add lines for the neck, legs and tail.

Step 2. Draw the foal's outline—notice that its back curves above the largest oval. Sketch in the face.

Step 3. Add details, as shown here. Include hooves, markings and a shaggy mane, and use short dashes to suggest fur. Go over your outline in pen, then erase the pencil guidelines.

Fact File

A male foal is called a colt and a female is called a filly. Foals are too young to be ridden.

Step 4. Complete your foal by coloring it in. Don't forget to highlight each eye with a small white circle.

Side-on View

Step 1. This guideline takes a bit of practice! Copy it carefully, taking care to get the angles and bends of the legs right.

Step 2. Go around your guidelines, sketching your foal's outline. Keep its back nice and straight.

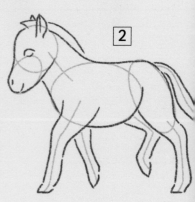

Step 4. Color in your cheerful foal. Give it a white blaze on its nose and white socks!

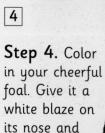

Step 3. Add detail to the legs, mane and tail, and give your foal markings and fur. Then go over your outline in black pen. Finally, erase the pencil guidelines.

Rabbit

Have fun drawing these cute fluffy bunnies from two angles!

Side-on View

Step 1. Sketch overlapping ovals for the body, head and fluffy tail. Add lines for the legs and ears.

Step 2. Next, draw the rabbit's outline and add the eye and nose.

Step 3. Draw the toes and use short dashes to suggest fur. Go over your outline in pen and erase the guidelines.

Step 4. Color in your bunny, leaving a white highlight in the eye.

Front-on View

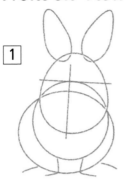

Step 1. Sketch an oval with a cross in it for the head. Add two overlapping ovals for the body, then draw the ears and lines for the legs.

Step 2. Draw your rabbit's outline around your guidelines. Next, sketch the face slightly off-center, so the rabbit looks as if it is watching something.

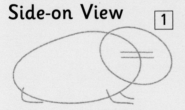

Step 3. Add detail to the face and feet, and lots of short strokes to suggest fur. Then go over your pencil lines in black pen and erase the guidelines.

Step 4. Color in your fluffy baby rabbit.

Fact File

A baby rabbit is called a kit. Rabbits are born blind and helpless. They spend their first ten days in a nest made from grass and soft fur.

Guinea Pig

Stocky little guinea pigs have great characters and make excellent pets.

Side-on View

Step 1. First, sketch two overlapping ovals for the head and body. Then add lines for the legs.

Step 2. Sketch your guinea pig's outline and draw in the folded ear and the eye, nose and mouth.

Step 3. Add markings, toes and short strokes to suggest fur. Then go over your outline in pen and erase the guidelines.

Step 4. Color in your furry friend. Don't be afraid to experiment with different colors!

Piglet

Here's your first farmyard animal—a snuffly piglet! Try it from two angles.

Fact File

A newborn piglet spends its time sleeping or suckling milk from its mother. It can double its weight in the first week!

Side-on View

1

Step 1. Start by sketching three overlapping ovals, plus four lines for the legs and a curl for the tail.

2

Step 2. Draw your piglet's ears and head, shaping the snout around the small oval. Complete the outline, taking care to shape the trotters.

3

Step 3. Add a few skin folds around the eye and front leg, then go over your outline in pen. Erase the pencil guidelines.

Step 4. Finish your drawing by coloring in your perky piglet!

4

Angled View

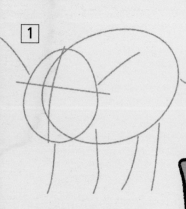

1

Step 2. Draw the piglet's outline around your guidelines, taking care to shape the ears and trotters. Position the left-hand ear and eye slightly higher than the right-hand ones. Add a slightly tilted nose and mouth.

2

Step 1. Lightly sketch a slightly tilted oval with a cross for the head and another oval for the body. Then draw lines to mark the position of the ears, legs and tail.

Step 3. Give your piglet a few skin folds. Then go over your outline in black pen. Erase any pencil guidelines.

3

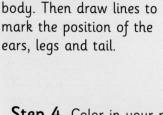

4

Step 4. Color in your piglet using various shades of pink. Some pigs have black patches, too!

Chick

Can you draw this fluffy chick?
It's just a few hours old!

Fact File

When chicks hatch out of an egg, they use a special tooth to peck away at their shell. It takes them several hours to hatch.

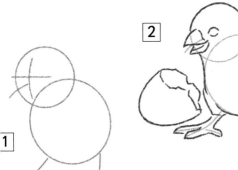

Step 2. Next, sketch your chick's outline. Draw in the beak and eye, and add two pieces of broken eggshell, as shown.

Step 3. Use short, diagonal strokes to suggest fluff on the head and body, and short lines on the legs and feet to suggest rough skin. Go over your outline in black pen. Erase any pencil guidelines.

Step 1. Lightly sketch a circle for the head and overlap it with another for the body. Add lines for the beak, legs and feet.

Step 4. Finally, color in the eggshell and the chirpy chick!

Donkey

Now try your hand at this gentle donkey foal.

Fact File

A female donkey, or Jenny, usually gives birth to just one foal—twins are very rare.

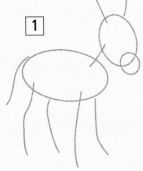

Step 2. Carefully draw the donkey's outline around your guidelines. Notice that the back curves above the large oval.

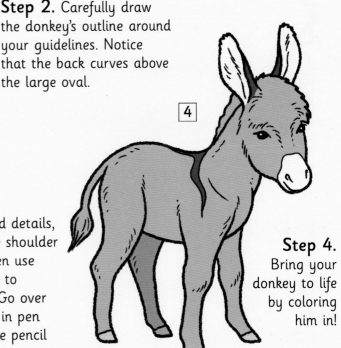

Step 1. Start by drawing two ovals for the head and one for the body. Add lines for the ears, neck, legs and tail. Try to copy the angles shown here.

Step 3. Add details, including the shoulder marking. Then use short strokes to suggest fur. Go over your outline in pen and erase the pencil guidelines.

Step 4. Bring your donkey to life by coloring him in!

Calf

A calf can see, stand up and walk as soon as it is born.

Fact File

A calf is fed milk for seven to nine weeks. It grows very quickly and is fully grown in a year.

Angled View

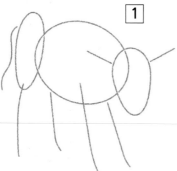

1

Step 1. First, create your guidelines by sketching three overlapping ovals for the head, body and rump, plus lines for the ears, legs and tail.

Side-on View

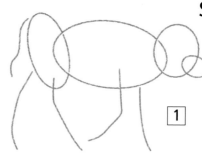

1

Step 1. For this side-on view, sketch four overlapping ovals plus lines for the legs and tail.

Step 2. Draw the calf's outline around your guidelines and sketch in the face.

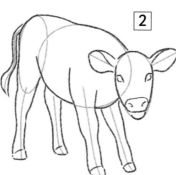

2

Step 2. Draw the calf's outline, starting with the head. Give him a nice straight back and shape his legs, as shown here.

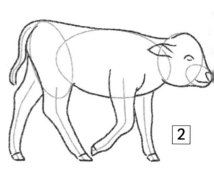

2

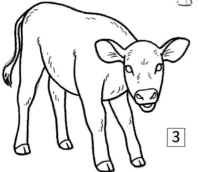

3

Step 3. Add further detail. Then, go over your pencil outline in black pen. Erase the pencil guidelines.

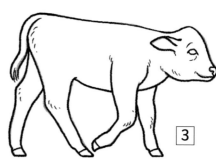

3

Step 3. Add some short strokes to suggest fur, and draw two lines around the eyes. G over your outline i pen and erase the pencil guidelines.

4

Step 4. Color in your calf. Don't forget to leave white highlights in the eyes.

Step 4. Color in your calf. You could even add some grass

4

...amb

...ee if you can draw this little lamb
...s it leaps towards you!

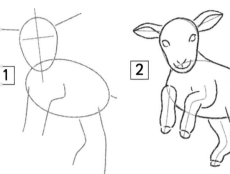

Step 2. Starting with the head, draw the lamb's outline. Then add its eyes, nose and mouth on its slightly tilted head.

Fact File

Lambs can stand on their feet soon after birth, but they are a little wobbly at first!

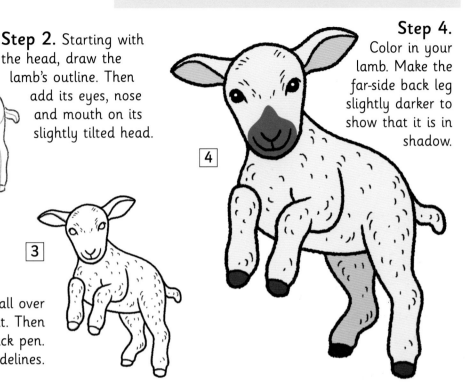

Step 4. Color in your lamb. Make the far-side back leg slightly darker to show that it is in shadow.

...tep 1. Lightly sketch the ...uidelines shown above, ...arefully copying the angles ...f the legs and ears.

Step 3. Draw little curved lines all over the lamb to suggest its woolly coat. Then go over your drawing in black pen. Finally, erase the pencil guidelines.

Duckling

...Here are two cute ducklings to draw!

...ront-on View

Step 1. First, draw these simple guidelines using three circles and some straight lines.

Step 2. Next, sketch the duckling's outline and give it an eye.

Step 3. In pen, re-draw the outline. Use short overlapping lines on the body to suggest feathers. Erase the pencil guidelines.

Step 4. Color in your fluffy duckling in shades of yellow and orange.

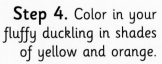

Fact File

Ducklings can swim from the moment they hatch, but they stay close to their mother for safety.

Side-on View

Step 1. Create your guidelines, as shown here. Try and match the angles.

Step 2. Draw the duckling's outline and give it an eye, a wing and wide webbed feet. Then draw the waterline.

Step 3. Use short dashes, as shown, to suggest feathers. Go over your outline in pen, and then erase the guidelines.

Step 4. Finally, color in your cute duckling!

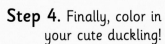

13

Fawn

A fawn will run away if it spots you. Can you draw this shy, gentle creature?

Fact File

Most fawns are born with white spots, but these may fade by the end of the fawn's first winter.

Side-on View

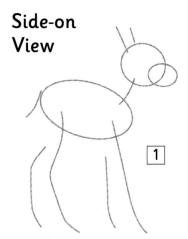

1

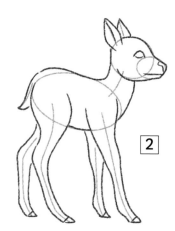

2

Step 1. First, sketch the guidelines shown above.

Step 3. Add some detail to the fawn's face and draw the spots. Then go over your picture in black pen and erase your pencil guidelines.

3

Step 2. Next, draw your fawn's outline around the guidelines, starting with the head. Notice that the back curves above the large oval.

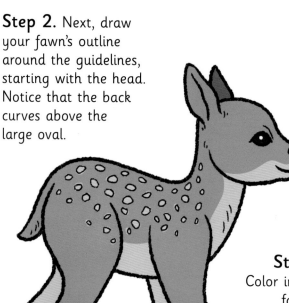

4

Step 4. Color in your fawn in shades of brown. Don't forget to leave a white highlight in the eye.

Angled View

Step 1. Start by sketching an oval for the head and a larger oval for the body. Add lines for the ears, neck, legs and tail. Try and copy the angles shown here.

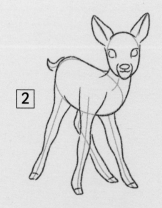

2

Step 3. Add the fawn's markings and some short dashes to suggest fur. Then go over your outline in pen. Erase the pencil guidelines.

4

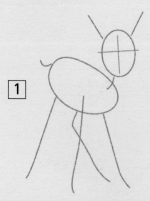

1

Step 2. Go around your guidelines drawing the fawn's outline. Take care shaping the legs, feet and ears. Then, draw the face.

3

Step 4. Color in your shy, long-legged friend.

Hedgehog

These prickly hedgehogs will really test your drawing skills!

Curled Up

1

Step 1. Sketch a large oval and draw two overlapping ovals inside it. Add lines for the feet.

2

Step 2. Draw the face and feet, and add spikes around the edges of the two body ovals.

3

Step 3. Add lots more spikes, including shorter ones on the face. Go over your drawing in black pen and erase the pencil guidelines.

4

Step 4. Color in your sleepy baby hedgehog.

Side-on View

1

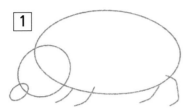

Step 1. First, sketch your guidelines by following the example above.

2

Step 2. Draw the outline. Take care when shaping the top of the head.

3

Step 3. Add the baby hedgehog's spikes. Notice that they lie flat at its back end. Then go over your outline in pen and erase the guidelines.

4

Step 4. Color in your spiky friend, leaving a white highlight in the eye.

Fox

A baby fox cub first leaves its den when it is about four weeks old.

Angled View

1

Step 1. Start by drawing a circle and small oval for the head. Add a large oval for the body and lines for the ears, legs and tail.

2

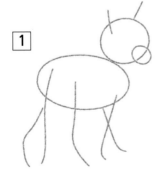

Step 2. Draw the fox's outline around your guidelines, and add the eyes and nose.

Step 3. Add short strokes to suggest fur. Then go over your drawing in black pen. Erase the pencil guidelines.

3

Step 4. Color in your alert little fox.

4

Meerkat

A meerkat "sentry" keeps guard while the rest of its group hunts for insects and spiders to eat.

Front-on View

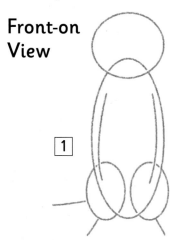

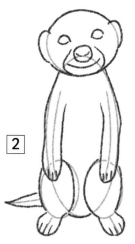

Step 1. For this simple guideline, sketch four overlapping ovals, as shown, and add lines to show the position of the front legs, feet and tail.

Step 2. Draw the meerkat's outline around your guidelines, and give your meerkat a smiling face. Remember to include ears!

Step 3. Add detail, such as markings, claws and short strokes to suggest fur. Then go over your outline in pen. Erase the pencil guidelines.

Step 4. Complete your baby meerkat by coloring him in!

Side-on View

Step 1. First, sketch a circle and small oval for the head. Overlap a large oval for the body, and add lines for the legs and tail.

Step 2. Draw your meerkat's outline around the guidelines. Add the ear, eye, nose and mouth.

Step 3. Build up the detail, sketching in the eye marking, claws and fur. Then go over your outline in pen and erase the pencil guidelines.

Step 4. Color in your bold little meerkat to complete the picture.

Lion

Practice a close-up face with this baby lion, then draw it taking its first steps!

Fact File

A mother lion usually gives birth to two or three baby lions, or cubs, in one litter.

Front-on View

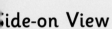

Step 1. Start by sketching a large circle. Draw a cross in the middle. Then add a smaller circle just below the crossbar.

Step 2. Draw the eyes on the crossbar, and use the smaller circle as a guide for drawing the nose and mouth. Add the two ears and the neck.

Step 3. Use short strokes on the face and around the edges of the outline to suggest fur. Add dots for whiskers. Then go over your drawing in pen and erase the pencil guidelines.

Step 4. Color in your cuddly baby lion. Don't forget to include white highlights in its beautiful blue eyes!

Side-on View

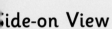

Step 1. For the side-on view of the lion cub, start by sketching two ovals. Then add lines for the neck, legs and tail, copying the angles shown here.

Step 2. Draw the lion's outline around your guidelines, taking care to get the line of the back right. Add detail to the face and ear.

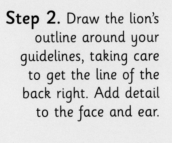

Step 3. Add more detail to the face and feet, and use short strokes to suggest fur. Go over your drawing in pen and erase the guidelines.

Step 4. Color in your lion cub, adding some faint brown markings.

Elephant

A wrinkly baby elephant makes a great subject to draw!

Fact File

An elephant calf drinks about three gallons of milk a day until it is about five years old.

Side-on View

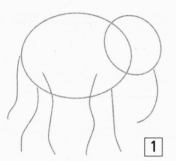

1

Step 1. Lightly sketch your baby elephant's guidelines by copying the example shown here. Try and match the angles of the legs.

Step 2. Next, draw the elephant's outline, starting with the ear, head and trunk.

2

Step 3. Work up the detail, such as tufts of hair on the head, toenails and wrinkles. Go over your drawing in pen, then erase the pencil guidelines.

3

Step 4. Color your baby elephant in shades of gray.

4

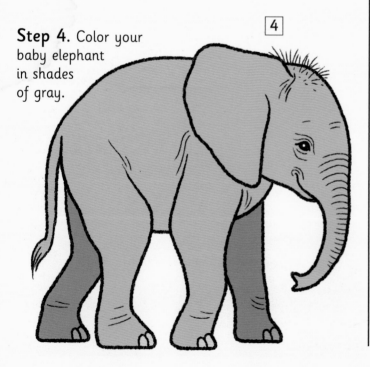

Angled View

1

Step 1. Start by drawing the guidelines for the head, ears and trunk, as shown. Then add the body and legs.

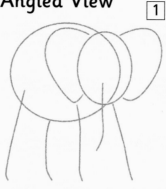

2

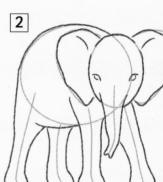

Step 2. Draw around your guidelines to build up the outline shape. Notice how the tummy curves below the larger oval.

3

Step 3. Add details such as eyelashes, wrinkles and toenails. Then go over your drawing in black pen. Finally, erase the pencil guidelines.

Step 4. To finish, color in your charming baby elephant.

4

Chimpanzee

Use these shapes to draw a chimpanzee. Take your time over each step!

Fact File

Chimps are clever creatures. They sometimes use sticks as tools to get food.

Chimp Side-on

1 **Step 1.** Copy the guidelines shown here, starting with the head.

Step 2. Draw the chimp's outline and face, then the near-side arm and leg and finally the far-side arm.

2

3

Step 3. Add the eyelashes, ear folds and shaggy hair. Then go over your picture in pen and erase the pencil guidelines.

4

Step 4. Color in your thoughtful baby chimp.

Front-on View

Step 1. Start by overlapping four ovals for the head. Then add a large oval for the body. Add lines for the arms and legs.

1

Step 3. Add the details shown here, including the skin folds in the ears. Go over your outline in pen and erase the pencil guidelines.

3

2

Step 2. Draw the chimp's outline and face. Take care shaping its long arms, fingers and toes.

Step 4. Color in your cheeky chimpanzee!

4

Tiger

This stripy tiger is terrrrrific to draw!

Fact File

During its first year, a tiger cub depends entirely on its mother for food. It stays with her until it is about two or three years old.

1

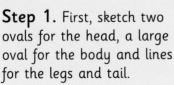

Step 1. First, sketch two ovals for the head, a large oval for the body and lines for the legs and tail.

Step 2. Draw around your guidelines to create the tiger's outline. Sketch in the ears, eye, nose and mouth.

2

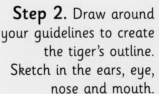

Step 3. Study the stripes before adding them to your tiger —notice which way they go. Then go over your outline in pen and erase the guidelines.

3

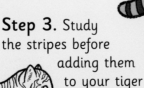

4

Step 4. Finally, have fun coloring in your stripy tiger cub!

Orangutan

Why not hang around with these cute baby orangutans and see if you can draw them?

Fact File

A female orangutan gives birth high in the treetops, or canopy. Her baby clings to her as she climbs through the branches.

Front-on View

1

Step 1. Sketch an egg-shape and a circle for the head. Overlap these with a large oval for the body. Add lines for the arms, legs and branch.

Step 2. Draw the outline around your guidelines, taking care to get the feet right. Add the eyes and ears (level with each other), then the nose and mouth.

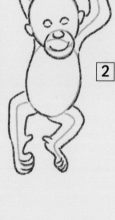

2

Step 3. Have fun adding the orangutan's long hair and wrinkles. Then go over your outline in pen. Erase the pencil guidelines.

3

Step 4. Color in your orangutan, giving the gray areas textured edges to suggest more hair.

4

Angled View

1

Step 1. First, sketch three overlapping ovals for the head and body. Copy the lines shown for the arms, legs and branch.

Step 2. Next, draw the baby orangutan's outline, starting with the head. Then add detail to the face.

2

Step 3. Use lots of long, curved lines for the hair, and add eyelashes, wrinkles and ear folds. Go over your outline in pen and erase the pencil guidelines.

3

Step 4. Complete your baby orangutan by coloring it in!

4

20

Panda

Giant pandas live in China. Like many animals, they are endangered.

Top Tip!

If you are drawing a slightly tilted head, sketch the features at the same angle as the rest of the face. Sketching a cross first will help!

Angled View

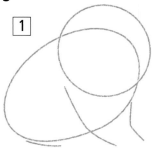

Step 2. Draw the panda cub's outline, adding ears and detail to the face. Place the eyes halfway down the face, quite close together.

Step 4. Color parts of your panda cub dark gray and leave white highlights in its black eyes.

Step 1. Create these simple guidelines for your panda cub. All you need is a circle, an oval and three lines.

Step 3. Add markings and fur, using short strokes. Go over your drawing in pen and erase the guidelines.

Side-on View

Step 1. Sketch two tilted ovals for the head, and a larger oval for the body. Add lines for the legs.

Fact File

In the wild, panda cubs are born in a den—usually a tree hollow or cave. After four to six weeks, they ride about on their mother's back.

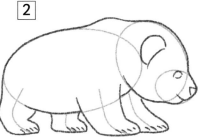

Step 2. Draw the panda cub's outline, giving it a hump at the shoulders. Add its large ear, face and claws.

Step 4. Color in your panda cub to finish!

Step 3. Draw in your panda's markings and add some short dashes to suggest fur. Then go over your outline in black pen before rubbing out the pencil guidelines.

Penguin

This plump penguin chick is quite easy to draw—why not give it a go?

Front-on View

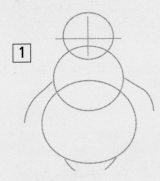

1

2

Step 4. Color in your plump, fluffy chick.

4

Step 1. Start by overlapping two circles and an oval, as shown. Add lines to show the position of the flippers and feet.

Step 2. Draw the chick's outline around your guidelines, and add detail to the face.

Step 3. Add more detail, including face markings, and short dashes to suggest feathers. Go over your sketch in pen and erase the pencil guidelines.

3

Angled View

1

Step 2. Using your guidelines, sketch the penguin's outline. Add the eye and beak.

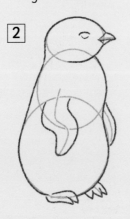

2

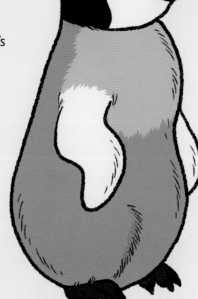

Step 3. Add markings and claws, and use short strokes to suggest fluffy feathers. Go over your outline in pen and erase the guidelines.

3

Step 1. Sketch three overlapping ovals for the head and body. Add lines to show the position of the beak, flippers and feet.

4

Step 4. Color in your chick with pens or pencils, remembering to highlight the eye with white.

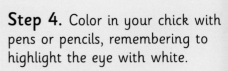

22

Otter

Test your drawing skills by doing two views of a playful baby otter.

Fact File

River otter pups are born in a den on land, and can swim after about two months.

Angled View

1

Step 1. In this view, the otter pup is looking up. Sketch the guidelines, as shown.

2

Step 2. Draw the pup's outline, then sketch the face. Because the face is tilted up, the features are higher on the head than usual.

3

Step 3. Add details, such as paws, whiskers and fur. Go over your outline in pen and erase any pencil lines.

4

Step 4. Color in your inquisitive little friend using shades of brown.

Side-on View

1

Step 1. Lightly sketch three ovals as guidelines for the head and body —try to match the proportions shown here. Then draw lines to show the position of the legs and tail.

2

Step 2. Draw the outline around your guidelines, carefully shaping the head. Add the ear, eye, nose, mouth and paws.

3

Step 3. Use short, curved strokes for the fur and add dots for whiskers. Work over your drawing in black pen, then erase the pencil guidelines.

Step 4. Color in your sleek, agile otter pup.

4

Seal

Wow your friends by drawing this adorable baby seal!

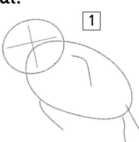

1

Step 1. Begin by drawing two ovals to represent the head and body. Add four lines for the flippers.

2

Step 2. Draw the seal pup's outline and face, and add detail to the flippers.

3

Step 3. Sketch in the whiskers and fur. Go over your outline in black pen and then erase the pencil guidelines.

4

Step 4. Color in your seal pup using shades of cream and gray. Include white highlights on the eyes and nose.

Conclusion

The more you practice, the easier your drawing will become.

Now that you have drawn all the pictures in this book, why not have a go at doing some stunning drawings of your own?

Choose a baby animal and spend time looking at it before you begin. Try to see it in your mind as a series of basic shapes. Study its proportions and angles.

Perhaps the most important thing to remember is to always draw what you can actually see, not what you think something looks like!

Now take out your sketch pad, pencils, a sharpener, an eraser and a pen—**and get drawing!**

Drawing Cartoons

You can have great fun using your new drawing skills to create cartoon baby animals!

The technique is the same as when drawing realistic baby animals, except that now you can have fun exaggerating body parts and giving your baby animal funny cartoon features.

1
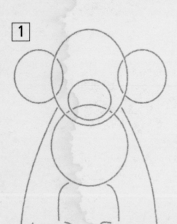

2

Step 2. Draw your chimp's outline around the guidelines, taking care to shape the hands and feet. As well as outsized ears, give your chimp extra-big eyes and hairy cuffs.

Step 1. Sketch an oval for your cartoon chimp's head, two large circles for the ears and a slightly smaller circle for the mouth/nose part of the face. Next, draw a large, overlapping circle for the body. Then add lines for the extra-long arms, short legs and toes.

3

Step 3. Have fun making your chimp cross-eyed, give it a funny mouth, and emphasize the ears by adding large skin-folds. Use short lines to suggest shaggy hair. Finally, go over your outline in pen and erase the pencil guidelines.

4

Step 4. Color in you comical, cross-eyed cartoon chimp